DISCOVERING
CENTRAL AMERICA

Belize

DISCOVERING
CENTRAL AMERICA

Belize

Charles J. Shields

Mason Crest Publishers
Philadelphia

Mason Crest Publishers
370 Reed Road
Broomall PA 19008
www.masoncrest.com

First printing

1 3 5 7 9 8 6 4 2

Library of Congress Cataloging-in-Publication Data
on file at the Library of Congress

ISBN 1-59084-092-5

CURR
F1433.2
.V43
.S54
2003

DISCOVERING
CENTRAL AMERICA

Belize
Central America: Facts and Figures
Costa Rica
El Salvador

Guatemala
Honduras
Nicaragua
Panama

Discovering Central America

James D. Henderson

CENTRAL AMERICA is a beautiful part of the world, filled with generous and friendly people. It is also a region steeped in history, one of the first areas of the New World explored by Christopher Columbus. Central America is both close to the United States and strategically important to it. For nearly a century ships of the U.S. and the world have made good use of the Panama Canal. And for longer than that breakfast tables have been graced by the bananas and other tropical fruits that Central America produces in abundance.

Central America is closer to North America and other peoples of the world with each passing day. Globalized trade brings the region's products to world markets as never before. And there is promise that trade agreements will soon unite all nations of the Americas in a great common market. Meanwhile improved road and air links make it easy for visitors to reach Middle America. Central America's tropical flora and fauna are ever more accessible to foreign visitors having an interest in eco-tourism. Other visitors are drawn to the region's dazzling Pacific Ocean beaches, jewel-like scenery, and bustling towns and cities. And everywhere Central America's wonderful and varied peoples are outgoing and welcoming to foreign visitors.

These eight books are intended to provide complete, up-to-date information on the five countries historians call Central America (Guatemala, El Salvador, Honduras, Nicaragua, Costa Rica), as well as on Panama (technically part of South America) and Belize (technically part of North America). Each volume contains chapters on the land, history, economy, people, and cultures of the countries treated. And each country study is written in an engaging style, employing a vocabulary appropriate to young students.

A watersports center at Journey's End, Belize.

All volumes contain colorful illustrations, maps, and up-to-date boxed information of a statistical character, and each is accompanied by a chronology, a glossary, a bibliography, selected Internet resources, and an index. Students and teachers alike will welcome the many suggestions for individual and class projects and reports contained in each country study, and they will want to prepare the tasty traditional dishes described in each volume's recipe section.

This eight-book series is a timely and useful addition to the literature on Central America. It is designed not just to inform, but also to engage school-aged readers with this important and fascinating part of the Americas.

Let me introduce this series as author Charles J. Shields begins each volume: *¡Hola!* You are discovering Central America!

(Opposite) The Xunantunich (Maiden of the Rock), a Mayan ceremonial center, overlooks the Hopan River in Belize. The Mayans flourished in the region, even after the arrival of Europeans in the early 16th century. (Right) A mangrove swamp in Ambergris Caye.

1 A Warm, Sultry Land Cooled by Sea Breezes

¡HOLA! ARE YOU DISCOVERING Belize? Belize is a land of majestic mountains, swampy lowlands, and tropical jungles. The name Belize comes from a Mayan word meaning "muddy water." But don't get the idea that this is a dismal land—not at all! The major industry here is tourism. This tiny, English-speaking country, free from political strife, features some of the best diving in the world, hundreds of Mayan ruins, and a gorgeous Caribbean coastline. Moreover, half of Belize is covered by deep forests that are home to many colorful and exotic animals. Formerly called British Honduras until its independence in 1973, Belize is well on its way to becoming one of the most popular destinations in Central America.

Geography That's Varied

Belize is located in the southeast of the Yucatán Peninsula on the Caribbean coast of Central America. In shape, Belize is roughly rectangular, measuring 173 miles (280 kilometers) from north to south and 67 miles (109 km) from east to west. It is bounded on the north and part of the west by Mexico, and on the south and the remainder of the west by Guatemala. The

Two men paddle their dugout canoe through a forest in the interior of Belize. Most of the country—about two-thirds, in fact—remains wild, unspoiled land.

principal streams are the Belize River; the Río Azul, which forms much of the boundary with Mexico; and the Sarstún River, which forms the south-western boundary with Guatemala.

Despite its small size, the geography of Belize is extremely varied. The country consists primarily of tropical lowland and swampy plains, though the Maya Mountains in the west rise to more than 3,300 feet (1,100 meters). Dense forests cover half the country. The remainder is farmland, *scrub*, and swamp. *Deciduous* trees are found in the north; tropical hardwood trees are common in the south. The types of trees that are commercially important in Belize include mahogany, cedar, and rosewood, as well as pine, oak, and palms. The forests provide habitats for many different kinds of animals, including jaguar, deer, puma, ocelot, armadillo, tapir, crocodile, and numerous species of reptiles. Keel-billed toucans can be found perched in tree branches as can an abundance of squawking macaws and parrots.

Belize by Region

The northern half of the mainland of Belize is a plain that was once the floor of a sea. As a result, the land has been exposed to air for only a short time in geological history, and is covered with just a thin layer of soil. Scrub vegetation grows here, and dense forest.

The central part of Belize consists of sandy soil that supports large *savannas*. Then, about 30 miles southwest of Belize City, the land rises toward the beautiful, deep green Mountain Pine Ridge Area and the Maya Mountains. The highest peaks rise up along the Cockscomb Range. Abundant rainfall runs off from the highlands into streams, which flow into the Macal River. The Maya Mountains and the Cockscomb Range become the backbone of the southern half of the country

The southern part of Belize contains numerous small streams that rush down slopes and hurtle over ledges and caves. The rivers, carrying sand, clay, and *silt*, enrich the coastal land, providing good soil for citrus and banana crops. Fed by heavy annual rainfall, southern Belize has a true tropical rainforest that is rich with ferns, palms, *lianas*, and tropical hardwoods.

Quick Facts: The Geography of Belize

Location: Middle America, bordering the Caribbean Sea, between Guatemala and Mexico.

Geographic coordinates: 17'15"N, 88'45"W

Area: (slightly smaller than Massachusetts)
total: 22,960 sq. km
land: 22,800 sq. km
water: 160 sq. km

Borders: Guatemala 266 km; Mexico 250 km; Coastline: 386 km.

Climate: tropical; hot and humid; rainy season (May to February).

Terrain: flat, swampy coastal plain; low mountains in south.

Elevation extremes:
lowest point: Caribbean Sea 0 m
highest point: Victoria Peak 1,160 m

Natural resources: arable land potential, timber, fish, hydropower.

Land use:
arable land: 2 percent
permanent crops: 1 percent
permanent pastures: 2 percent
forests and woodland: 92 percent
other: 3 percent
Irrigated land: 20 sq. km

The low coastal area is a sodden, swampy belt barely separating land from sea. *Mangrove*, long grasses, cypress, and sycamore trees flourish here. The coastal waters of Belize are stunningly clear and shallow, sheltered by a line of coral reefs. The coast is also dotted with over 1,000 islets called "cayes" (pronounced the same as "keys"), extending almost the entire length of the country. Nineteen miles (30 km) offshore lies the world's second largest barrier reef—185 miles long. The cayes, the offshore *atolls*, and the barrier reef are the main attractors for tourists to Belize.

Although swampy mangrove cayes are normally unsuitable for humans, they provide a superior habitat for birds, fish, shellfish, and other marine life. Long-legged herons and snowy egrets can be seen wading through the warm waters of mangrove swamps, for example, spearing fish with their long beaks. The sandy island cayes, on the other hand, shaded by palm trees, are ideal for tourist resorts. Diving, snorkeling, fishing, boating, sailing, sail boarding, sea kayaking, and bird and animal watching attract sports-minded persons and naturalists alike. Beyond the barrier reef, the continental shelf ends abruptly in a drop-off that sinks to over 10,000 feet.

Hot and Breezy Weather

The climate of Belize is subtropical. A brisk breeze from the Caribbean Sea blows regularly across the coast. In summer, the temperature rarely exceeds 96° F (35.5° C), and winter lows are rarely below 60° F (15.5° C), for an average temperature of 79° F (27° C). The sea water temperature ranges between 75° and 84° F (24° to 29° C)—warmer than most outdoor pools.

The warm, shallow waters off the coast of Belize are ideal for scuba diving, snorkeling, and other water sports. The second-largest barrier reef in the world, a popular tourist attraction, is 19 miles off Belize's seacoast.

There are more than a thousand small islands, or cayes, stretched along Belize's Caribbean coast.

Annual rainfall ranges from 50 inches in the north to an amazing 170 inches in the south. The rainy season is usually between June and August, and the dry season is between February and May. At the end of October, the weather becomes cooler, and from November to February, rain showers swing through during the afternoons. The average humidity is 85 percent, which makes for warm and sultry weather in Belize in general.

This ornate Mayan carving (opposite) depicts a sun and water god. (Right) A Mayan youngster holds her baby sister. At one point in its history, millions of Maya lived in Belize; their descendants remain in the country today.

2 A History Different from the Rest of Central America

THE ANCIENT HISTORY of Belize is similar to that of its Central American neighbors, but Belize's modern history is quite different. A branch of the powerful Mayan civilization flourished in the region. But the Spanish empire, which came to Central America during the 16th century, never established a strong foothold. As a result, no European conquest displaced the Amerindian population. Instead, English settlers and peoples from the Caribbean created a culture apart from the rest of Central America.

Puritans and Pirates

The Mayan civilization spread into the area of Belize between 1500 B.C. and A.D. 300 and flourished until about A.D. 1200. Archaeologists estimate that at their peak, 1 to 2 million Amerindians lived within the borders of present-day Belize. Several major archaeological sites, such as Caracol, Lamanai, Lubaantun, Altun Ha, and Xunantunich, were once great Mayan towns with farmland between them. No one knows for certain what caused the disappearance of the Maya. Perhaps it was war, loss of faith, famine, or a series of natural disasters. Eventually, the civilization declined, leaving behind small groups whose descendants continue to live mainly in Belize and Guatemala. By the time the Spanish arrived in the 16th century, many of the Mayan cities were deserted.

European contact began in 1502 when Christopher Columbus sailed along the coast. He did not come ashore, however, only naming the bay bordering the southern part of the giant barrier reef the Bay of Honduras.

The first recorded European settlement in the region happened accidentally. In 1638, a band of shipwrecked English sailors landed on the shore. Later, English Puritans established trading posts on the coast, just as fellow Puritans had already done in New England. Over the next 100 years, more English settlements were established, although a rougher breed of settler

Christopher Columbus explored the coast of present-day Belize during his fourth and final voyage to the New World in 1502. Within 25 years the Spanish had established settlements throughout Central America—with the exception of Belize.

gradually replaced the Puritans. Most of these men were English, Scottish, and Irish *buccaneers*. Many were former British soldiers and sailors, disbanded from military service after the capture of Jamaica from Spain in 1655. They took to calling themselves "Baymen," after the Bay of Honduras. In their ragtag ships, they struck out at passing Spanish *galleons* loaded with gold, silver, and hardwoods.

The British Gain Control

Although the Spanish considered themselves the "owners" of Belize because they controlled nearby Mexico and Guatemala, they did not actually rule it. From time to time, they tried to expel the troublesome Baymen, but failed. In 1763 and 1786, Spain signed treaties permitting settlers in the region to continue cutting valuable trees like mahogany and logwood (used in making dye) in exchange for protection from piracy.

In 1798, however, while Spain and Britain were at war, a Spanish fleet roamed the coast, pounding villages with cannon-fire. In a sea battle off St. George's Caye, British ships, aided by Baymen and slaves, defeated the

> ## Did You Know?
> - Belize's flag is royal blue with one horizontal red stripe at the top, one at the bottom, and a white circle with the coat of arms in the center; the motto *Sub Umbra Florero* on the coat of arms means "under the shade (of the mahogany tree) I flourish."
> - The national tree of Belize is the mahogany tree.
> - The national flower of Belize is the black orchid, which grows on trees in damp areas, and flowers nearly all year round.
> - The national bird is the keel-billed toucan, noted for its great, canoe-shaped bill and brightly colored green, blue, red, and orange feathers.
> - Belize's national animal is the tapir, or mountain cow, the largest land mammal of the American tropics.

enemy, delivering Belize from Spanish rule. Following the independence of all Central America from Spanish rule in 1821, the British claimed the right to administer Belize in 1836. Britain completed its hold by declaring British Honduras, as it was then called, "a Crown colony" in 1862. The United States, too deeply involved in the Civil War to enforce the terms of the *Monroe Doctrine*, grudgingly accepted the change, and the Crown colony system of government was introduced in 1871, with a legislature presided over by a lieutenant governor appointed by the British.

A Unique Identity Takes Shape

In the second half of the 19th century, a unique identity evolved for Belize. European settlers married freed slaves, forming the Creole majority—still the largest part of the current population. Mexican citizens began cultivating small farms in northern Belize. To the south, the Kekchi and Mopan Maya retreated to the hills of the Maya Mountains. A small band of American Civil War veterans from the defeated Confederate army settled in what is now Punta Gorda. From the Bay Islands of Honduras, the Garifuna people migrated and settled along the coast of Belize. Also known as Black Caribs, the Garifuna are descendants of Caribbean islanders and black slaves used by the Spanish in the 1600s as farm laborers and woodcutters.

By the early 1900s, Belize had grown to nearly 40,000 inhabitants. However, the economy was poor. In 1931, a hurricane destroyed Belize City, and throughout the 1930s, the economy was so poor that the residents began to call for independence. After World War II, Belize's economy weakened still further.

Because of Belize's location on the Caribbean Sea, it is subject to devastating hurricanes and tropical storms. These homes in Placencia, a village to the south of Belize's capital, Belmopan, were destroyed by Hurricane Iris. The storm left 13,000 people homeless when it hit in October 2001.

The Road to Independence

In 1961, Britain declared it was prepared to assist Belize on the road to independence, although Belize would remain part of the British Commonwealth, like Canada or Australia. Democratic political parties formed, and self-government was granted in 1964. A new capital at Belmopan was constructed in 1970 because a second hurricane had all but destroyed Belize City in 1961.

Guatemalans watched Belize's progress toward independence angrily. They felt the territory should become part of their country. In 1972, Guatemala threatened war. Despite this, the official name of the region was changed from British Honduras to Belize in June 1973. When Belize finally attained full independence on September 21, 1981, Guatemala refused to recognize the new

This young Creole girl lives in Belmopan, the capital of Belize. About 13,000 people live in Belmopan, which became the capital after a hurricane devastated Belize City in 1961.

nation. About 1,500 British troops remained stationed in Belize to protect it from invasion by Guatemalan troops.

During the 1980s, while civil wars raged in Guatemala, El Salvador, and Nicaragua, Belize remained stable due largely to financial assistance from the United States. In 1992, a new Guatemalan government recognized Belize's territorial right to exist, and the two nations forged diplomatic ties. The British soldiers were withdrawn in 1994. Today, Belize has a standing army of only a few hundred soldiers.

Belize is a ***parliamentary democracy***, modeled on England's, and is a member of the British Commonwealth. Queen Elizabeth II is head of state and is represented in the country by a governor general. The primary executive branch of government is the cabinet, led by a prime minister (head of government). Cabinet ministers are members of the majority political party in Parliament and usually hold elected seats in the National Assembly in addition to their cabinet positions. The National Assembly consists of a House of Representatives and a Senate.

(Opposite) This hideaway in Ambergris Caye is said to have been used by the famous buccaneer Henry Morgan, an English pirate of the late 17th century. Morgan attacked Spanish shipping, as well as Spanish settlements. His greatest accomplishment was sacking Panama City in 1671. (Right) A man climbs a sapodilla tree to gather chicle, to be used for chewing gum.

3 Careful Land Use Strengthens the Economy

FOR CENTURIES, THE economy of Belize was based on forestry, mainly the export of logwood, mahogany, and chicle—a tree whose fruit can be used in making gum and ice cream. Today, the country's economy centers on agriculture. Belize is rich in farmable land, but only a fraction of it is being used for pasture or crops. With so much available land, the government of Belize has made developing agriculture a *priority*. Ranking second in importance is encouraging more tourism. To accomplish that goal, however, better roads, transportation, and resort areas will be needed.

Farmable Land: The Best Asset

Belize's main economic resource is its farmable land. About 38 percent of Belize is suitable for agriculture, but only 10 percent is under *cultivation*. About half of this is used as pasture, with the rest going for permanent and annual crops. More than one-third of Belize's workers are agricultural workers.

Earlier in its history, Belizean farmers used a system called *milpa*—clearing new land for crops or pasture as soils wore out (this practice was also used in colonial America). In recent years the Department of Agriculture in Belize has mounted a campaign to teach farmers how to replenish the soil with fertilizer. More farmers are using tractors and other mechanical means, too, to maximize the yield of their orchards and fields.

In Belize, rice, beans, and corn are grown as *subsistence* crops—that is, foods grown primarily to be eaten by the local people. Agricultural exports from Belize to other countries include sugar, citrus fruits, and bananas. Dairy farming is growing in importance, and the livestock industry continues to grow, too. Efforts are being made to encourage Belizean farmers to grow a greater variety of

A Belizean corn farmer in San Miguel. About 33 percent of the people of Belize work in agriculture.

crops, rather than rely too much on the sale of a few foodstuffs. Almost three-quarters of the country's income from trade comes from food exports alone, one-third of which comes from just sugar.

To prevent the price of land from being driven too high by foreign real estate developers, the government enacted a special law in 1973. Non-Belizeans must file a development plan—how they intend to use the property—before obtaining ownership to plots of more than 10 acres of *rural* land, or more than one-half acre of *urban* land. The purpose of the law is to maintain a balance between developers of tourist resorts and Belizean citizens who depend on the land for their livelihood.

Fisheries and Forestry

Belize has a small, but thriving, fishing industry. The most popular seafood sold for export are lobster, conch shells, finfish, aquarium fish, stone crab claws, shrimp, and shark. Some of these appear on menus in local restaurants, too, along with smoked fish. There are laws to protect the rock lobster (also called the spiney lobster) to avoid overfishing. Lobster fishing is not allowed between March and July. Export markets for fish are mainly in the United States, Mexico, and Jamaica. The Belize Fisheries Department was established in 1965 to help manage this natural resource.

Forestry was the only major economic activity in Belize until well into the 20th century. Then, the supply of timber began to dwindle. Recently, though, forestry has been making a comeback in Belize. *Reforestation* in the pine forests and creating nurseries for fast-growing tropical hardwood trees are becoming common practices.

Tourism on the Rise

A combination of natural factors—climate, the longest barrier reef in the Western Hemisphere, numerous islands, excellent fishing, safe waters for boating, jungle wildlife, and Mayan ruins—support Belize's increasingly important tourist industry. In 1999, for example, tourist arrivals totaled 181,000 (more than 85,000 from the United States) and tourist receipts amounted to $108 million. A small number of airlines provide service to Belize—American Airlines, Continental Airlines, and Latin American Grupo Taca Airlines from gateways in Dallas, Houston, Miami, and San Salvador.

Riding horses is a popular activity for tourists around San Ignacio. More and more, tourism is becoming an important part of Belize's economy.

Quick Facts: The Economy of Belize

Per capita income (2001): $3,100
Natural resources: farmland, timber, seafood, minerals.
Industry (17 percent of GDP*): clothing, fruit processing, beverages.
Agriculture (16 percent of GDP): sugar, citrus fruits and juices, bananas, mangoes, papayas, honey, corn, beans, rice, cattle.
Tourism (67 percent of GDP)
Foreign trade (2001): Exports $183 million: cane sugar, clothing, citrus concentrate, lobster, fish, bananas, and farmed shrimp.
Major markets: United States, 43 percent; United Kingdom, 30 percent; Central American Common Market, 15 percent; Mexico: 12 percent.
Unemployment rate (1999): 14.3 percent.
Economic growth rate (1999): 6.4 percent
Currency exchange rate (2003): 1 Belizean dollar = U.S. $1 (fixed rate)

* GDP or gross domestic product—the total value of goods and services produced in a year

Industry, Investment, and Trade

A number of manufactured or produced goods come from Belize: metal doors and windows, furniture, concrete blocks, bricks, clothing, boats, beer, cigarettes, flour, animal feed, wire and paper products, agricultural fertilizer, matches, plywood and other wood products, meat packing, food processing, and rolled steel bars for the construction industry.

In addition, the United States Embassy in Belize City lists 185 U.S. companies with operations in Belize, including MCI, Duke Energy International, Archer Daniels Midland, Texaco, and Exxon (Esso).

Even so, tourism attracts most foreign investors, who build hotels and resorts, although investors from the United States have also become involved in Belize's energy, telecommunications, and agriculture industries.

Belize continues to rely heavily on foreign trade, with the United States as its number one trading partner. Total imports from the United States in 1999 totaled $370 million, while total exports were only $183 million. Other major trading partners include the United Kingdom, European Union, Canada, Mexico, and member states of the Caribbean Common Market (CARICOM).

Belize's economy depends a great deal on world prices for its goods. Downward trends in the prices of sugar and bananas, for instance, with its trading partners the United States and Britain, can have a major negative effect that ripples throughout the country's economy. This is the main reason why the government encourages farmers to raise a variety of crops.

Better Roads and Utilities Needed

An obstacle to economic development in Belize is the lack of what is called "infrastructure investments"—money to maintain roads, bridges, housing, highways, and so on. A road network of 1,785 miles (2,872 km) links the major urban centers, but some areas remain closed to vehicles. During the rainy season, some roads, including sections of major highways, are closed.

In 2001, the government undertook a multimillion-dollar attempt to improve the roads, repair highways, and construct two major bridges. A second campaign is underway to upgrade health centers and hospitals throughout Belize. The government also plans to invest $50 million in building low-income houses.

A boy walks down a dirt road near the Mayan ruins at Lubaantun. Belize will have to upgrade its network of roads throughout the country in order for its economy to grow during the 21st century.

Although electricity, telephone, and water utilities are all relatively good, Belize has the most expensive electricity in Central America due to a lack of power plants.

More than half of Belize's total *revenue* comes from customs *duties* on imported goods. Ports in Belize City, Dangriga, and Big Creek handle regularly scheduled shipping from the U.S. and Britain, although *draft* for ships is limited to a maximum of 10 feet in Belize City and 15 feet in southern ports.

To continue its economic progress, Belize depends on financial aid from other countries. The government also encourages foreign investment to create jobs.

(Opposite) Dawn breaks over Belize City, the largest city in the country. Nearly 20 percent of the nation's population—just over 49,000 people—lives in this city, which at one time was the capital of Belize. (Right) A man rakes a clear path through the jungle near Chan Chich.

4 A Mosaic of Backgrounds and Languages

BELIZE IS THE MOST sparsely populated nation in Central America. Slightly more than half of the people live in rural areas. The greatest concentration of the population is in Belize City, the principal port, commercial center, and former capital. Most Belizeans are of multiracial descent. Many Belizeans, more than one-third, are black or of partly black ancestry. Six languages are commonly spoken in the various towns and villages.

A Small Population of Mixed Peoples

In 2001, slightly more than one-quarter million people lived in Belize. The overall density of 29 persons per square mile (11 persons per sq. km) is the lowest in Central America. This is because, first, the total number of

33

people living in Belize is small, and second, most people live in a few principal urban centers.

Nearly a fifth of the population lives in Belize City (49,050 persons in 2000), which is also the principal port. The next largest urban area is Belmopan (13,260 persons in 2000). Belmopan replaced Belize City damaged by a hurricane in 1961, as the official capital in 1972. Belmopan is located inland on high ground, practically in the geographic center of the country, about 50 miles (80 km) to the southwest of Belize City. Its population is increasing as more people, mainly government workers, continue to relocate to the new capital. Outside of these two small cities, the Belizean countryside is largely open with scattered villages.

According to a recent census, the main ethnic groups in Belize are *mestizo* (mixed white and Amerindian), Creole (mixed white and black), Maya (Yucatec, Mopans, and Kekchi Amerindians), and Garifuna (mixed black and Caribbean islander).

Other ethnic groups account for a small percentage of the population: East Indian, German/Dutch, and Mennonite. Large neighborhoods of Arabs, Europeans, and Chinese can be found, too. In the late 1990s, Belize tended to be a refuge for Guatemalans fleeing fighting between guerrillas and government forces. Figures from January 1997 show that 8,672 registered refugees had settled in Belize. Since then, many have returned home.

Mestizos

Mestizo are a Spanish-speaking people descended from Yucatec Maya and Spanish. The first *mestizo* migrated from the Yucatán peninsula of

Mexico during a period of civil war in the mid-19th century. *Mestizo* were the founders and are still the majority population of Caye Caulker in Belize.

Creoles

Creoles are a mixture of European, African, and other groups. The Creole language is widely spoken in Belize. It is derived from rapidly spoken English, uses Spanish vowel sounds, and has its own grammar.

Two-thirds of the Creole population resides in Belize City. After slavery ended, Creole men rose to positions of authority in the logging industry. Today, political parties and media—television, newspapers, and radio—tend to be dominated by people of this background.

The Garifuna

The Garifuna are descended from Carib and Arawak Indians who intermarried with escaped Africans from two slave ships that sunk in the eastern Caribbean in the 17th century. By the late 1700s, they lived apart in communities on the islands and shores of Central America. In 1802, some came to Belize from the Bay Islands of Honduras. Today, the Garifuna are clustered in the southern towns of Punta Gorda and Dangriga, as well as the villages of Seine Bight, Hopkins, Georgetown, and Barranco. Some also reside in Belize City and Belmopan.

Fishing and agriculture are traditional ways of life for the Garifuna. Rituals and traditions are important to them as they strive to maintain a distinct place in Belizean society. November 19 is a national holiday in Belize commemorating the arrival of the Garifuna on the shores of Belize in 1802.

A group of Kekchi Amerindian children show off crafts they have made. The Kekchi are a subgroup of the Maya, the native tribe that dominated Belize throughout most of its history.

Quick Facts: The People of Belize

Population: 249,183

Ethnic groups: 44.1 percent *mestizo*; 31 percent Creole; 9.2 percent Maya; 6.2 percent Garifuna; 9.5 percent other.

Age structure:
0–14 years: 43 percent
15–64 years: 54 percent
65 years and over: 3 percent

Population growth rate: 2.75 percent

Birth rate: 32.29 births/1,000 population

Death rate: 4.81 deaths/1,000 population

Infant mortality rate: 25.97 deaths/1,000 live births

Life expectancy at birth:
total population: 70.91 years
male: 68.66 years
female: 73.28 years

Total fertility rate: 4.14 children born per woman

Religions: 62 percent Roman Catholic, 30 percent Protestant, other or none, 8 percent.

Languages: English (official), Spanish, Mayan, Garifuna (Carib), Creole, German.

Literacy: 70.3 percent

*All figures 2002 estimates, unless otherwise noted.

The Maya in Belize

Belize was the home of the earliest Mayan settlements. Archaeologists have found traces in Belize's Orange Walk District of Mayan communities that date as far back as 2000 B.C. It is estimated that around 1 million Maya populated Belize at one time, but today there are only about 30,000.

There are three groups of Mayan Amerindians in Belize: the Yucatec, Mopan, and Kekchi Mayas. The Yucatec originated from Yucatán, and came to Belize in the mid-19th century, fleeing civil war in Mexico. Most can be found today in the Corozal and Orange Walk districts. The Yucatec Mayas in Belize mainly speak English and Spanish instead of their native

Did You Know?

- Belize's government is a parliamentary democracy. The head of state is Queen Elizabeth II (since February 6, 1952). She is represented in Belize by Governor General Sir Colville Young (since November 17, 1993). The head of Belize's government is Prime Minister Said Musa, who was appointed on August 27, 1998.
- There are no elections in Belize. The monarchy is hereditary; the governor general is appointed by the monarch; and the governor general appoints the prime minister from the House of Representatives. This is usually the leader of the majority party.
- The National Assembly consists of two houses: the Senate (eight members, five appointed on the advice of the prime minister, two on the advice of the leader of the opposition, and one by the governor general; members are appointed for five-year terms); and the House of Representatives (29 seats; members are elected by direct popular vote to serve five-year terms).
- Belize has a Supreme Court; the chief justice is appointed by the governor general, with the advice of the prime minister.

language. Likewise, their traditional rituals have given way to Christian beliefs.

The Mopan Mayas, fleeing forced labor on plantations, came to Belize in 1886 from Peten. They live mainly in San Antonio Village in the Toledo District and other villages in the Cayo District.

Kekchi Mayans came to Belize in the 1870s, also to escape forced labor. They settled in Belize's lowland areas along rivers and streams, forming small isolated villages throughout the Toledo District. Because of their isolation, the Kekchi have the reputation of being the most self-reliant ethnic group in Belize. They are also known as a peaceful people who farm cooperatively.

The Mennonites

The Mennonites, originally from Russia and Germany in the 19th century, immigrated to Belize from Mexico and Canada in the late 1950s. They reside in the Orange Walk and Cayo districts in six villages: Blue Creek, Shipyard, Little

A group of young Mennonite men from an orthodox sect gather on a dirt road in Belize. The Mennonites emigrated to Belize during the mid-20th century. They have established their own schools, banks, churches, and businesses.

Brothers carry home a load of firewood near Maya Centre, Belize.

Belize, Progresso, Spanish Lookout, and Barton Creek. Their clothing easily identifies Mennonites. Women wear bonnets and long dresses, and the men wear denim overalls and wide, floppy hats.

The Mennonites have made it a point to have their own schools, churches, and financial institutions in their farming communities. Their vegetables, dairy, and poultry are sold in stores throughout the country. Belizeans and tourists alike favor handcrafted Mennonite furniture.

English the Official Language

English, the official language, is spoken by nearly all Belizeans, except Central American refugees who arrived during the past decade. Spanish is the native tongue of about 50 percent of the population, and is spoken as a second language by another 20 percent.

The Garifuna, Mayans, and Mennonites speak their own languages in addition to English and Spanish. The various Mayan groups speak their original languages, which can be traced back more than 1,000 years. Creoles speak an English-Creole dialect (or "Kriol"), similar to the Creole dialects of the English-speaking Caribbean Islands and southern Louisiana in the United States. Mennonites speak German.

Did You Know?

- Belize received its independence from Great Britain on September 21, 1981.
- The capital of Belize is Belmopan.
- The voting age is 18.
- Major political parties include the People's United Party (PUP) and United Democratic Party (UDP).

(Opposite) A cruise ship steers around the edge of the Blue Hole, an unusual natural formation on Belize's Lighthouse Reef. The deep hole leads to a series of underwater caves and caverns. Local legends say it was the home of a sea monster. (Right) The Rio On forms a cataract in Belize's Mountain Pine Ridge Forest Reserve.

5 Communities and Cultures Clustered by Districts

THE BEST WAY TO understand Belize's culture is to focus on separate areas of this tiny nation. Belize is divided into districts, each of which tends to reflect the mix of people living there. In addition, Belize's natural history and archeological sites are distinctive. With the support of organizations such as the Audubon Society, the Smithsonian Institute, the World Wildlife Fund, and many zoological societies, Belize hosts a variety of preserves and sites worth visiting.

Corozal District

Corozal is the northernmost district of Belize and borders the Mexican city of Chetumal. It is a coastal district, inhabited mostly by *mestizo* and

Locals congregate at a corner market in San Pedro, Ambergris Cay.

Yucatec Mayas. The most important city of this district is Corozal Town, perched on the edge of the Caribbean Sea. The town is approximately 96 miles up the Northern Highway from Belize City. The ancient Maya ruins are major attractions of the districts, such as those at Santa Rita. Tourists come to see wildlife *lagoons* in this district, too. Shipstern Nature Reserve, for example, features a hardwood forest, savanna that is home to deer, tapir, and other wildlife, and 25 species of butterflies. The economy of the Corozal is based on raising sugar cane, papaya, and fishing.

Orange Walk

Orange Walk is the secondmost northern district. *Mestizo*, Yucatec Mayas, and Creoles live here. Many Chinese and Hindus own shops and restaurants. The major city of the district is Orange Walk Town, located 54 miles up the Northern Highway from Belize City. Its major activity is the production of sugar cane. Sugar cane trucks rumble with their loads into Orange Walk Town constantly. Lining Yo Creek Road on the outskirts are large sugar cane plantations. Other important economic activities are cattle rearing and vegetable growing. Important attractions in Orange Walk include the Maya ruins at Lamanai, El Posito, Cuello, Nohmul, Chan Chich, and the Rio Bravo Conservation Area.

Reefs and Resorts

Along the coast in this part of Belize are a number of natural attractions. Ambergris Caye is a long, slender island stretching north to south, just inside the famous 185-mile barrier reef, for almost 25 miles. The nearness of Ambergris Caye to the reef makes it a favorite destination of divers and fishermen alike. Water visibility often reaches 100 feet, and water temperature hovers between 75° F and 84° F. The barrier reef makes for calm water most of the year.

For fishing, the *estuaries*, inlets, and mouths of many rivers along the coast are known for tarpon, snook, and jacks (these are types of fish). The lagoons and grass flats are fished for bonefish. The coral reefs support grouper, snapper, jacks, and barracuda. The deep waters beyond the drop-off of the continental shelf are home to sailfish, marlin, bonito, and pompano.

The Turneffe Islands cluster in this part of Belize, forming an atoll. The interior lagoon is a maze of mangrove-lined channels and tiny uninhabited cayes. Offshore, at both the north and south ends of the atoll, beautiful reefs and dramatic walls offer incredible diving with great visibility. Lighthouse Reef is a part of the atoll's oval reef structure and is home to a nesting colony of endangered, rare red-footed boobies. A fascinating phenomenon for divers at Lighthouse Reef is the Blue Hole. A mammoth-size cave, once dry, as evidenced by *stalactites*, has been submerged since the Ice Age. A portion of its ceiling collapsed at some time, forming an underwater hole more than 400 feet deep and nearly 1,000 feet in diameter.

The Cayo District

The Cayo District is in the midwestern part of the country. A mixture of *mestizo* and Central American immigrants who came to Belize escaping the civil wars in their own countries live here. Santa Elena and San Ignacio are twin towns in the Cayo District, scenically located in a hilly area near the Maya Mountains. High above the towns is the Mountain Pine Ridge, a forest preserve. Nearby, the Caracol Mayan Temple, recently excavated, may have been the center of power in the region long ago. In the Cayo District, citrus growing, grains, and cattle are the main economic activities.

Stann Creek District

Stann Creek is a coastal district inhabited mostly by Garifunas, descendants of Caribs from the island of St. Vincent. Its most important city, Dangriga, is known as the City of Culture, since the people are rich with its Garifuna music and dances characterized by the beating of drums.

The Stann Creek Valley gives the district its distinct characteristic shape and natural beauty, formed by the chain of surrounding mountains. Driving on the Hummingbird Highway from Belmopan to Stann Creek, the shape of the Sleeping Giant can be seen, formed by the hills on the on the edge of the valley. The Cockscomb Jaguar Reserve on the eastern side of the Maya Mountains is a major attraction for ecotourists. The major economic activities in this area are fishing, bananas, and citrus growing.

Toledo District

Toledo is the southernmost district of the country. Many people would say that Toledo is the forgotten district because of its poor roads and limited communication system. On the other hand, most of its forest remains untouched. Its natural resources, combined with the rich culture of the Maya, makes Toledo District the perfect place for the development of ecotourism. Punta Gorda Town is the main city and the commercial center of Toledo. It is a fairly small town on the shore of the Caribbean Sea. Mayan communities can be found in this district, as can communities of East Indians and Garifunas.

Rivers and Kayaking

Though Belize is a relatively small country, with low-lying land, it receives plenty of rain during the winter season and supports 20 major river systems and smaller streams. These many waterways hold potential outdoor adventures for the kayak and canoe lovers. This is an excellent way to bird watch and view wildlife along the banks, too.

Bird Watching and Wildlife

Because of Belize's small population and lack of industry, much of Belize has remained virtually undisturbed. About two-thirds of the country

An overview of Chan Chich Lodge, near the Rio Bravo Conservation Area in Belize's Orange Walk district.

is still forested. Birdwatchers have the opportunity to observe hundreds of different species of birds. It is not uncommon to view 50 in a single outing. Belize has recorded over 500 species of birds within its borders. Any of the national parks make excellent locations from which to bird watch. Of special interest are Cockscomb Basin Wildlife Sanctuary, Crooked Tree Wildlife Sanctuary, Silk Grass Creek Road, and Mountain Pine Ridge.

> ## Did You Know?
>
> These are the official holidays in Belize.
> - January 1—New Year's Day
> - March/April—Good Friday, Easter
> - May 1—Labor Day
> - May 24—Commonwealth Day
> - September 10—St. George's Caye Day
> - September 21—Independence Day
> - October 12—Columbus Day
> - November 19—Garifuna Settlement Day
> - December 25—Christmas Day
> - December 26—Boxing Day

Wildlife is a little more difficult to view, especially the jaguar. Most animals see, smell, hear, or feel a human long before the human is aware that an animal is nearby. However, the Belize Zoo is a good place to be sure of seeing local exotic animals.

A Borrowed Cuisine

Belize has never really developed a national cuisine. Its cooking borrows elements from Britain, the United States, Mexico, and the Caribbean. The traditional staples are rice and beans. These are often eaten with chicken, pork, beef, fish, or vegetables. Coconut milk and fried plantain add a tropical flavor. Exotic traditional foods include armadillo, venison, and fried paca, a small rodent similar to a guinea pig.

A Calendar of Belizean Festivals

February

One week before Lent, the **Fiesta de Carnaval**, an annual traditional event, is celebrated nationwide. Groups compete in *comparsas* (special dances).

The **International Bullfish Tournament** offers a prize of $50,000 to any angler who lands a blue marlin over 500 pounds. Sponsored by the Belize Game Fish Association.

The **San Pedro Carnival**, a traditional *mestizo* carnival, features competing *comparsas*. Participants use powder, flour, lipstick, and paint to disguise each other.

March

The annual **Agricultural & Trade Show** is held in Belmopan, Orange Walk Town, and nearby Chan Pine Ridge every two years. It features livestock, handicrafts, traditional costumes, and dances.

Celebrations are held on **Baron Bliss Day** to honor the British nobleman who willed his fortune to Belize. A regatta is held in the harbor in front of the lighthouse where his grave is located. Horse and cycle races are also held.

Every other year, on the last weekend in March, the **Trade & Livestock Show** is held in Belmopan at the National Agricultural Showgrounds. It features a rodeo.

April

Because most residents of Belize are Christian, there are many festivities surrounding the season of Lent, Holy Week, and Easter Sunday. On Good Friday in Ambergris Caye and Caye Caulker, special Catholic Church services are held. Most villagers participate in processions carrying a crucifix through the streets.

On Holy Saturday, the **Cross Country Classic**, a bicycle race that draws participants from all over the world, is held in Belize City.

The **San Jose Succotz Fiesta** is a local fair celebrating the day of the town's patron saint. Entertainment for children, as well as rides, food, and marimba music are offered.

May

The **Cashew Festival** is held in Crooked Tree Village to celebrate the cashew harvest season. It features live punt music, cashew wine, Caribbean-style dishes, games, and folklore stories.

Cayo Expo, held in San Ignacio, offers displays of local crafts and products, as well as samples of local foods.

Caye Caulker's **Coconut Festival** features a parade with prizes for floats, coconut competition, and dancing, as well as food and beverages.

Commonwealth Day is celebrated nation-wide as the Queen's birthday. The National Sports Council holds horse races in Belize City at the National Stadium and in Orange Walk Town at the People's Stadium. Cycle races take place between Cayo and Belmopan.

On **Labor Day**, an address by the Minister of Labor or a representative is followed by parades and rallies. Other activities include kite-flying contests, cycle race, harbor regatta, and horse races.

A Calendar of Belizean Festivals

In Toledo, the weeklong **Festival of Arts** features school children depicting various cultural groups through drama and music. Arts and crafts exhibition includes basketry, paintings, clay sculpture, seashells, and calabash vessels.

June

An early-morning boat parade begins **Dia de San Pedro**, a three-day festival honoring St. Peter, the patron saint of San Pedro. Priests bless boats and fishermen during a special mass.

July

A local fair, the **Benque Viejo del Carmen Fiesta**, celebrates the day of Benque Viejo del Carmen's patron saint with cultural shows, marimba bands, food, and games.

August

The **Deer Dance Festival**, held in San Antonio, features weeklong celebrations, historical reenactments, costumes, and homemade harps and violins.

The **International Sea & Air Festival** in San Pedro is a festival of music, dance, and foods from Belize, Mexico, and neighboring countries.

September

Independence Day is celebrated with numerous cultural, religious, and sporting activities, flag-raising ceremonies, parades, street jump-ups, music, dance, and foods. A festival is held for the crowning of Miss San Pedro.

In Orange Walk and Corozal during **Mexican National Day**, townspeople cross over into Mexico to reunite with families and celebrate.

St. George's Caye Day commemorates a battle in 1798 when the Spanish were defeated by slaves, Baymen, and British soldiers. Carnivals, sporting activities, fire engine parade, and pop concerts held several days prior to this event.

October

The **Belikin Spectacular**, a bullfish tournament with prizes, is sponsored by the Belize Game Fish Association.

On October 12, **Columbus Day** (also called **Pan American Day**) is celebrated with regatta racing in Belize City. Fiestas and beauty contests are held in Orange Walk and Corozal to celebrate *mestizo* culture. Horse and cycle races are held as well.

Hike & Bike for the Rainforest, a two-day cross-country run and mountain bike race for the benefit of the rainforest, draws both local and international athletes to the Cayo area.

November

Garifuna Settlement Day is a festival held mainly in the southernmost areas of the country to mark the first arrival of the Garifuna in 1832 in Dangriga.

The **Stann Creek Agricultural Fair** features exhibits of livestock and locally grown fruits and vegetables.

December

Boxing Day features parties, dances, horse races, and Garifuna dances.

Recipes

Orange Eggnog

(Serves 2 to 3)
1 cup cold milk
1 egg
1/2 cup orange juice
1/2 tsp. vanilla
1 tsp. powdered sugar

Directions:
Mix all ingredients in bowl, and beat for two minutes with an eggbeater. Serve.

Sweet Potato Pone (Pudding)

(Serves 10 to 12)
3 lbs. sweet potatoes
1/2 cup butter
2 lbs. sugar
2 14-oz. cans coconut milk
1 14-oz. can evaporated milk
1 Tbsp. vanilla
1/2 cup raisins
2 Tbsp. grated ginger

Directions:
1. Preheat oven to 350° F.
2. Grate sweet potatoes.
3. Add sugar and coconut milk.
4. Stir until sugar dissolves, then add evaporated milk, butter, vanilla, and raisins.
5. Stir until thoroughly mixed, and pour into a 9 x 11 inch baking pan. Bake for 45 to 60 minutes.

Carrot Coconut Bread

(Serves 6 to 8)
3 eggs
1/2 cup cooking oil
1 tsp. vanilla
2 cups finely shredded carrots
1 cup sugar
2 cups flour
1/2 tsp. salt
2 tsp. salt
2 tsp. baking powder
1 tsp. cinnamon
2 cups grated coconut
1 cups raisins

Directions:
1. Preheat oven to 350° F.
2. In a large bowl, beat the eggs until light. Stir in cooking oil and vanilla. Add carrots, coconut and raisins, and mix until well blended.
3. Combine the flour, salt, baking powder, cinnamon, and sugar. Sift into the first mixture. Stir until well blended.
4. Spoon into loaf tin that has been well buttered and dusted with flour. Bake in oven for about 1 hour.
5. Remove from tin, and cool thoroughly. Its flavor and texture improves if wrapped and refrigerated for several days.

Avocado Eggnog

(Serves 2 to 4)
3 eggs, separated
1/2 tsp. salt
1 Tbsp. honey
2 cup milk
1 Tbsp. grated orange peel
1/2 cup avocado, peeled, seeded, and mashed

Directions:

1. Beat egg yolks with milk and avocado. Add honey, orange rind, and salt. Blend well.
2. Beat egg whites until stiff, and fold into milk mixture. Dust with nutmeg.

Rice and Beans

(Serves 4)
1 cup red kidney beans
1 cup canned coconut milk
1 clove garlic (optional)
2 cup cooked rice
1 onion, sliced
salt and pepper to taste

Directions:

1. Combine all ingredients into a large pot.
2. Heat slowly until the liquid is absorbed (try not to boil the coconut milk).
3. Fluff rice gently with a fork.

Honey Candy

(Serves 8 to 10)
1 lb. honey
1/2 lb. sugar
2 oz. butter

Directions:

1. Boil ingredients until a glob hardens when dropped in cold water.
2. Turn out boiled ingredients into shallow plates. Be careful, as this will be hot.
3. When cool enough to handle, twist or work into desired shapes.

Glossary

Atoll—a coral island consisting of a reef surrounding a lagoon.

Buccaneer—a pirate who preyed on Spanish ships in the West Indies during the 17th century.

Cultivation—planting, growing, and harvesting crops or plants, or preparing land for this purpose.

Deciduous—leaf shedding; having leaves that turn color and fall off seasonally.

Draft—the depth of water a ship must have to float while loaded.

Duty—a tax on goods, especially imports and exports.

Estuary—a water passage where a sea tide meets a river current.

Galleon—a heavy square-rigged sailing ship of the 15th to early 18th centuries used for war or commerce.

Lagoon—a shallow channel or pond that feeds into a larger body of water.

Liana—a woody vine found in tropical rainforests that roots in the ground.

Mangrove—tropical trees or shrubs that send out many twisting roots, which build land in coastal areas.

Monroe Doctrine—United States' foreign policy that does not permit European control or influence in the Western Hemisphere.

Parliamentary democracy—a system of government in which a legislative body is responsible for making the laws. The people elect the members of Parliament.

Priority—of first importance.

Reforestation—replanting trees in great numbers.

Revenue—sources of income, such as taxes, that a country receives into its treasury for public use.

Rural—in the countryside.

Savanna—a tropical or subtropical grassland containing scattered trees.

Scrub—a stunted tree or shrub.

Silt—fine-grained sediment, especially of mud or clay particles washed from a river or lake.

Stalactite—a deposit of calcium carbonate hanging from a stone ceiling like an icicle.

Subsistence—necessary for life.

Urban—having to do with a city.

Project and Report Ideas

Maps

- Create an ecology map of Belize. First, draw the shape of the country, adding major rivers and mountains. Then, in the margins, put pictures of the trees and animals mentioned in chapter one. Under each, write a sentence of descriptive identification.
- Draw a map of the coast of Belize. Identify major reefs, atolls, and cayes. Define what these natural features are.

Book Reports

Write a one-page book report on any of the following titles:

Timothy of the Caye by Theodore Taylor

The Cay by Theodore Taylor

A General History of Pyrates by Daniel Defoe (Manuel Schonhorn, editor)

Under the Black Flag: The Romance and the Reality of Life Among the Pirates by David Cordingly

Flashcards

Using the glossary in this book, create flashcards. Put the term on one side and the definition on the other. Practice with the cards in pairs. Then, choose two teams of three. Select a referee to say the term out loud, and then call on someone to give the definition. The referee's decision is final. Award points for each correct answer. You can also read the definition, and ask for the correct term instead!

Projects

- Using a picture of a Mayan temple, build a small-scale model or show what one of the famous sites looks like from the air.
- Using a picture again, re-create a Mayan glyph using model clay. A glyph is a symbolic figure or character carved into something, for example, stone. Make it about the size of a textbook lying flat.
- Choose either the plants or animals of Belize and make mobiles of them to hang in class.

Cross-Curricular Reports

• In teams, assemble a list of the best Web sites for finding out about Belize. Devise a rating system. Include a one- or two-sentence summary about the site. Combine these sites into a comprehensive guide to Belize on the Internet for other classes to use.

• Write one page, five-paragraph reports answering any of the following questions. Begin with a paragraph of introduction, then three paragraphs—each developing one main idea, followed by a conclusion that summarizes your topic:

> Why did the great Mayan civilization fade in the regions of Belize and Guatemala?
>
> Who are "ecotourists?" What kind of vacations might they have?
>
> How are giant reefs created? Why are they important?
>
> How do tropical fish come from oceans to pet stores? (Do an Internet search using the keywords "tropical fish.")
>
> What is the British Commonwealth? Who belongs to it? How does it operate?
>
> How does reforestation take place? Is it happening in the United States?

Classroom Fiesta

If your city, town, or village was going to have an annual festival that captured some of the best things about where you live, what should be included? In small groups, choose examples of:

> Local, popular, or traditional food
>
> Local or regional music (country/western, jazz, religious, etc.)
>
> Exhibitions of local crafts or hobbies (fishing, soccer, baseball, gardening, etc.)
>
> Displays of symbols in your area: the city seal, the school mascot, the mascot of the favorite professional sports team, the religious symbols used outside of churches and temples, etc.
>
> Illustrations of native wildlife—commonly seen plants and animals.

Chronology

1500 B.C.	The Mayan civilization spreads into the area of Belize and flourishes until about A.D. 1200.
1502	Christopher Columbus sails along the coast of Belize and names the Bay of Honduras.
1638	A band of shipwrecked English sailors lands on the shore.
Late 1600s	Puritans and pirates settle the coast.
1763	Spain signs a treaty permitting settlers in the region to continue cutting down valuable trees.
1786	A second treaty is signed between settlers in the Belize area and Spain.
1798	The British navy, aided by Baymen and slaves, drives off the Spanish fleet in a sea battle off St. George's Caye.
1821	Central American countries declare independence from Spanish rule.
1836	Britain claims the right to administer Belize.
1862	Britain completes its hold by declaring British Honduras, as it was then called, "a Crown colony" in 1862.
1871	The Crown colony system of government is introduced.
1961	A hurricane destroys Belize City, the capital.
1972	Belmopan becomes the new capital of Belize; Guatemala threatens war unless its territorial claims on British Honduras are respected.
1973	Official name of the region is changed from British Honduras to Belize.

1981 Belize attains full independence from Britain, although it remains part of the British Commonwealth.

1992 Guatemala recognizes Belize's territorial right to exist.

1994 The British garrison of soldiers stationed to protect Belize withdraws.

2001 Belize's population reaches a quarter million, up from 40,000 at the beginning of the 20th century.

2002 Latin American leaders, including Belize's prime minister, Said Musa, meet in Argentina for the Global Alumni Conference to discuss technological and economic issues.

Further Reading/Internet Resources

Brown, Dale M., editor. *The Magnificent Maya*. New York: Time-Life Books, 1998.

Henderson, James D. *A Reference Guide to Latin American History*. Armonk, N.Y.: M. E. Sharpe, 2000.

May, Antoinette. *The Yucatán: A Guide to the Land of Maya Mysteries plus Sacred Sites at Belize, Tikal and Copan*. San Carlos, Calif.: World Wide Publishing/Tetra, 1993.

Meyer, Franz O. *Diving & Snorkeling in Belize*. Houston: Pisces Books, 1998.

Morrison, Marion, and George I. Blanksten. *Belize*. Chicago: Children's Press, 1996.

Staub, Frank J. *Children of Belize*. Minneapolis, Minn.: Carolrhoda Books, 1997.

Woodward, Ralph Lee Jr. *Central America: A Nation Divided*, 3rd ed. New York: Oxford University Press, 1999.

Travel information

http://www.belizenet.com
http://www.lonelyplanet.com/destinations/central_america/belize/
http://www.travelbelize.org

History and Geography

http://lcweb2.loc.gov/frd/cs/bztoc.html
http://www.belize.gov.bz/belize/welcome.shtml
http://search.ebi.eb.com/ebi/article/0,6101,32271,00.html#033577

Economic and Political Information

http://www.state.gov/www/background_notes/belize_0400_bgn.html
http://www.cia.gov/cia/publications/factbook/geos/bh.html

Culture and Festivals

http://www.belizeexplorer.com
http://worldtwitch.virtualave.net/belize.htm

The Belize Audubon Society
P.O. Box 1001
12 Fort Street
Belize City, Belize
Central America
011-501-2-35004

Belize Tourism Board
New Central Bank Building, Level 2
Gabourel Lane
P.O. Box 325
Belize City, Belize
011-501-2-31913
1-800-624-0686
info@travelbelize.org
www.travelbelize.org

Caribbean/Latin American Action
1818 N Street NW
Washington, D.C. 20036
202-466-7464

The Embassy of Belize in the United States
Ambassador James Schofield Murphy
2535 Massachusetts Avenue NW
Washington, D.C. 20008
202-332-9636

The Embassy of the United States in Belize
P. O. Box 286
Belize City, Belize
Central America.
011-501-2-77161
embbelize@belizwpoa.us-state.gov

U.S. Department of Commerce
International Trade Administration
Office of Latin America and the Caribbean
14th & Constitution NW
Washington, D.C. 20230
202-482-1658

Index

Contributors

Senior Consulting Editor **James D. Henderson** is professor of international studies at Coastal Carolina University. He is the author of *Conservative Thought in Twentieth Century Latin America: The Ideals of Laureano Gómez* (1988; Spanish edition *Las ideas de Laureano Gómez* published in 1985); *When Colombia Bled: A History of the Violence in Tolima* (1985; Spanish edition *Cuando Colombia se desangró, una historia de la Violencia en metrópoli y provincia*, 1984); and co-author of *A Reference Guide to Latin American History* (2000) and *Ten Notable Women of Latin America* (1978).

Mr. Henderson earned a bachelors degree in history from Centenary College of Louisiana, and a masters degree in history from the University of Arizona. He then spent three years in the Peace Corps, serving in Colombia, before earning his doctorate in Latin American history in 1972 at Texas Christian University.

Charles J. Shields, the author of all eight books in the DISCOVERING CENTRAL AMERICA series, lives in Homewood, a suburb of Chicago, with his wife Guadalupe, an elementary-school principal. He has a degree in history from the University of Illinois in Urbana-Champaign, and was chairman of the English department and the guidance department at Homewood-Flossmoor High School in Flossmoor, Illinois.